Kristian.

Thank you for supporting The Balance Book. I pray that this 21 day guide supports you on your personal wellness journey.

The Balance Book

21 Days of Motivation & Meditation

Lanasia Angelina

Published by:
Claire Aldin Publications
P. O. Box 453
Southfield, MI 48037
www.clairealdin.com

Cover Design by: Jackie Zimmerman www.QueenofGSD.com

Library of Congress Control Number: 2020910084
ISBN: 9781734746907 (paperback)

Printed in the United States.

Dedication

I want to dedicate this book to every single "no" that hurt like hell in the moment, but propelled me forward in the direction of my purpose. To every fear that tried to stop me that I turned into fuel for my fire; I thank you. For every single disappointment, misfortune, sickness of the mind and sadness of the heart that weighed so heavily on me at one point that I almost gave up; but instead used it as wood to keep my fire burning...I thank you.

Because of fear, I was granted the opportunity to exercise my faith. Because of being lost in the wilderness, I was given the opportunity to discover who I was and where I was. Because of past failures, I am now able to confront and conquer self-doubt. Personal success is not a destination, but instead it's a journey; comprised of new discoveries of the world around you and of the world that within you. Because of my discoveries, I eventually began to experience life in abundance and all thanks goes to every single thing that was designed not to stop me, but instead to strengthen me.

Ecclesiastes 3:1-8 NIV

There is a time for everything,

And a season for every activity under the heavens:

A time to be born and a time to die,

A time to plant and a time to uproot,

A time to kill and a time to heal,

A time to tear down and a time to build,

A time to weep and a time to laugh,

A time to mourn and a time to dance,

A time to scatter stones and a time to gather them,

A time to embrace and a time to refrain from embracing,

A time to search and a time to give up,

A time to keep and a time to throw away

A time to tear and a time to mend

A time to be silent and a time to speak

A time to love and a time to hate

A time for war and a time for peace

Introduction

When you picked up this book you were probably expecting to learn about work-life balance, time management, organizational skills and the cookie cutter steps to perfectly maintaining healthy relationships and a successful career at all times. Unfortunately, I don't believe that any of that is even possible. I don't even believe that people are searching for balance. Not at all. I believe that people are searching for the best strategies to help them successfully navigate the inevitable imbalances within specific areas of their lives, including work and interpersonal relationships.

Contrary to popular belief, there is in fact, no such thing as work-life balance, only **life** balance. I also believe that the balance doesn't begin with the routine, the true balance begins within the mind. Do you believe that you have the ability to properly manage and maintain the wealth and wellness within your life?

I titled this book *The Balance Book* because it's a day and night devotional designed to assist you with your commitment to better managing these specific areas. This is how the balance that everyone is chasing becomes a possibility. Taking realistic steps to resolve issues that have gone un-addressed, discovering power and potential that remains untapped is what we are all really searching for.

My hope for everyone who reads this book and completes this 21-day self-coaching process is that you have the opportunity to face your fears, shift your mindset and discover your greatness. I want you to create balance by improving the management of the most critical aspects of your life. I want you to experience YOUR balance, whatever that looks like for you. I want you to find clarity throughout this journey as you raise your awareness to your emotions, behaviors and imaginations.

You will work to achieve life balance with intention. Each day, you will experience a balance of motivation & meditation of a familiar concept in a brand new way by challenging the way you've imagined it before. Motivate yourself daily through methods of commitment and enthusiasm. Meditate each night through methods of reflection and relaxation. Your experience will be unique to you; immerse yourself in it.

A Note from the Author

I decided to structure each day of this journey by into two parts because I believe that it reinforces the concept of commitment. Regardless of what you will face after each morning motivation, no matter what happens throughout each day, you will be met with another opportunity to get back on track each evening.

This book is all about balance. Often we have motivational speakers encouraging us to give 100% each day, go hard, drive fast, and press past your limits. I agree that all of these things will help you to achieve external success. The intensity of speakers like Eric Thomas (ET), The Hip Hop Preacher, is necessary, but for the right time. You also need the peaceful, powerful Ghandi's of the world, who encourage you to have that same 100% go hard energy, yet applied with alternative, yet still very effective, methods.

I wanted so badly to live up to the standards of the motivational speakers who encouraged me to give 100% each day, go hard, drive fast and push past my limits. But when the days came that I felt completely overwhelmed and just needed to rest, those motivational videos that I listened to each day were in fact having a negative impact on self-esteem due to my literal interpretation of them.

When any average "do-gooder" gets tired, they just rest, but I wanted to be extraordinary and for some reason, I associated lack of rest with greatness. If I was a little tired, I'd feel like a total failure; I'd affirm how lazy I was and I'd beat myself up because there was no way that I could ever achieve success if I slept, right? No one should ever feel bad about themselves for being tired. Yes, it is very important to have a sense of self-awareness that helps you to identify abnormalities in your diet, sleeping habits and just general moods throughout the day. But if you're awake 18-20 hours and you just so happen to yawn, try not to panic. Instead find the nearest place to relax your mind and your body for the next six hours at least. Of course, ideally, most would like to have the non-stop Energizer bunny mentality where you don't require sleep. I'm sure, not much to your surprise, you have enough of an understanding to know that you are actually a human being…one who is not a toy designed specifically for a marketing ad. Unlike that toy bunny, the human body NEEDS rest; the mind NEEDS rest.

In fact, the busier I made myself with work, the more hours I spent proving that I was a "doer" and the less productive I found myself becoming. Movement and progress are not synonymous. It wasn't until I began to be intentional about my peace, about setting aside time to work and setting aside time to rest that I truly brought my life into balance. Sadly, like those motivational speakers were encouraging me to do, I was giving 110% but I was giving it to all of the wrong things at the wrong times. I was driving extremely fast with no direction and I was pushing past my limits without probable cause. I had to choose between a lifestyle of failure that sometimes looked good to others because contrary to the quote "a picture says a thousand words", it doesn't. Although my pictures were screaming success, **I was failing**. It was only once I chose a life of sacrifice that I experienced the growth that would stretch me in a direction of achievement. Now, don't get me wrong; failing is a necessary, character building part of the process, but I also knew that it was a part of the process that gave me two options every time. There was the opportunity to change my method and direction or continue on the path that would increase the likelihood of me experiencing the same failures over and over again. I refused to be stuck with the latter. I refused to give up. I refused to be so overwhelmed by 2 p.m. that I was paralyzed in bed with the weight of my thoughts and emotions keeping me bound…not because I was a failure, but because that wasn't the truth. I wasn't guilty of being a failure. I was guilty of was mismanaging my time, mismanaging my thoughts and mismanaging my emotions.

I knew that I had to do something quick or I'd continue to drive myself insane because of the imbalance that I had created within my own life. Just as I was creating schedules and to-do's so that I could succeed within my business, I realized that I had to be intentional about succeeding in my personal life, as well. I had no desire to be a person who had obtained financial wealth but was absent of spiritual wellness.

This balance is necessary in allowing us to take more deep breaths and restore ourselves through prayer and meditation. The strength that we actually possess is a direct reflection of an inner strength which can be developed with intention. This is what you should invest even more time into maintaining, which is a goal of the daily and nightly sessions. Treat these sessions as if I am right there coaching you each time.

By implementing meditation practices, consistent prayer and healthier daily habits, you, too can become more productive. I began properly prioritizing my agenda so that I could maximize my time; doing the difficult things first and knocking out the small tasks with ease. I also stopped staying up late hours just to post on social media about how I was working so hard on my laptop; PSA - No one cares about your MacBook boomerang at 2 a.m.

Adequate rest allowed me to wake up before the sun without an alarm clock. I was accomplishing every task on my agenda because instead of having 20 busy things to do, I now only had three important things that I was accomplishing every single day. Accomplishing my goals resulted in my self-esteem improving and me becoming more effective for not only my business, but for the people around me. I had more time to build and maintain healthy relationships and naps became an enjoyable thing once again instead of pure agony and torture.

This peace, joy, and forward motion didn't come overnight. These things were all a result of focused effort, consistency and most importantly, awareness. Before anything would change I had to **become aware** of what thoughts and habits needed to change, **acknowledge** that they were not serving me, **take action** to create a change and hold myself **accountable** for long-term success. I affirmed the things I wanted to have and the person I wanted to become. I developed a habit of awareness, of my toxic thoughts and emotions as they arose inside my mind and heart and I began to practice combating them immediately with opposing truths. I took better care of my health by working out daily, even if it was just a 30-minute walk. I was eating food that actually had nutritional value, soaking up more sunlight, laughing more often, and accomplishing my goals both personally and professionally. I became more aware of the music I allowed into my life, people, television, and content on my social media. I created in my life a *culture* of success; successful thoughts, successful habits, successful surroundings because success is not a destination, it is a lifestyle that you are responsible for creating.

As you and I take this journey of guided motivation and meditation over the next twenty-one days, I am praying that the words on the lines of these pages help you to increase your level of consciousness. My hopes are that you laugh, cry, and strip away every ounce of pain, doubt, and unforgiveness to restore everything that is within you, develop every asset, and rebuild what was once destroyed. I also want you to keep in mind four things:

1. **It is important that you give 100% each day, but it's even more important when you've depleted your battery that you recharge. Let me explain:**

Think of yourself as your prized possession like an iPhone. If you have an Android then just imagine that you have an iPhone and how much of a prized possession it would be. Anyway, my first time ever purchasing an iPhone, I remember the sales representative explaining all of the incredible features of my new phone to me. He showed me cool things that my phone did besides scroll social media five hours a day and take 30 pictures until I got the perfect angle. But within that presentation, the sales rep emphasized the importance of letting my phone's battery die completely at least once every 30 days to get the best charge.

Disclaimer: Not sure if this still applies today, but these were the directions in my 3G days. For the sake of the point that I am trying to make, we'll roll with it.

In no way would I ever suggest that you literally die. The point that I am trying to make is that the best version of yourself is revealed after you have allowed all negative energy, negative thoughts, and toxic choices to die. You will never experience the fullness of life as long as you are allowing yourself to be drained by thoughts and things that no longer serve you.

2. Practice doesn't make perfect; it makes progress.

It is my mission to eradicate the idea that perfection is anything beyond becoming. A combination of consistency of movement, rate of speed and efficiency is what creates perfection. Forward movement is synonymous with perfection. Resilience is perfection. Growth is perfection. There is no cookie cutter lifestyle that everyone should strive to achieve and there is definitely no road map that you can follow to get to your destination. Success is not linear. The learning, the growing, the falling, the pain, the effort, and the giving are all perfect pieces which create the ultimate portrait of perfection.

Let's redefine perfection for ourselves. I can say with certainty that either you have used the phrase or you've heard someone else use the phrase *"I'm not where I want to be, but I've come so far."* Why do we minimize our progress by comparing it to an unattainable goal like perfection? Any goal that you have, I challenge you to measure it on an attainable scale. If you are trying to lose weight, celebrate when you've loss 50 pounds, or 20 pounds, or even five pounds, as long as the metric for success that you've created for yourself is something that you can actually accomplish within a specific time frame; whether you meet the mark or not. As long as perfection is on the opposite end of the scale, you'll never arrive.

3. **Your peace is just as more important as your financial prosperity, if not more, but never less.**

I will keep this one short and sweet. What does it profit a man to gain this world and but to lose his soul (Mark 8:36)?

The answer... Absolutely nothing!!

The experiences worth living for are not the ones that you can hold in your hands but rather the ones that you hold within your heart. As you hold these experiences, they make you better. They teach you how to love. They give you the permission to be free. They stretch you to reach your true potential that will allow you to fulfill your purpose and your pockets, without having to sacrifice one for another.

4. **You are in control of your imagination.**

If you imagine that your life is one of wealth and wellness then you have given that imagination permission to become your reality. The same goes for imagining the worst case scenario. Your thoughts shape your world. What do you want to see in your world? I suggest you align your thoughts with those manifestations.

5. **When you begin to search for what you need, make sure you look inside first.**

You are lacking nothing. Everything that you need is already within. You have a well of untapped potential. Fear, doubt and comparison are dream killers! Do not allow yourself to succumb to these thoughts. The commitment that you need is there. Find it and activate your greatness.

Throughout this journey, there will be a few principles that I swear by within my own life that I hope will also assist you. These principles are as follows:

- **Rules:** This is where you take the time to be intentional about separating the negotiable from the non-negotiable. It is imperative that you do not live a life on the fence about anything. Straddling the fence feels safe until you realize that your feet aren't touching the ground. Eventually you have to make a decision and choose a side so that you can become grounded to begin walking in a direction that is in fact conducive to your success on any level. As you read this book and join this experience, make hard and fast decisions. Some will, obviously take more time but the goal is to create a habit of decisiveness. This will help to build your confidence in your own decision making abilities. Trust yourself.

- **Reflection:** In every season and in every situation, you are granted the opportunity to either enjoy it or to endure some discomfort that forces you to grow. Life is not just a feel-good experience. It is a learning experience, so don't overlook the value in each situation. That situation was designed to assist you in achieving goals in the next level or season of your life.

- **Realness:** This term is used so loosely and the term's association varies across different cultures. In urban communities, it is often associated with "realness" in vernacular and style. Within the Christian community, realness is often associated with how you worship and choose to live, but these things are on a surface level. The realness that I want you to experience throughout your journey is the realness that allows you to strip away everything which has been a result of you not being completely honest with yourself.

There are individuals who take pride in their ability to be forthcoming with others about their shortcomings. What I've come to realize is that those same people who express so much courage in their candidness with others have the most difficulty in being forthcoming with themselves. How do I know this? Because I was that person. I was once the most critical person I had ever met. I would criticize everyone else's clothes, shoes, cars, speech, decisions, or anything that I could focus on that would keep the focus off of me having to be *real*. I hated in others the things that I hated within myself. Essentially, I wasn't being real; I wasn't being honest. I was running away from the truth that was necessary for me to face because it was easier to point out the shortcomings of everyone else, as long as it meant that I didn't have to deal with my own.

One of the truest statements I've ever heard is 'every time you point the finger at someone else, you still have three more pointing back at you'. This is a mantra that I live by now. It helps to keep me accountable. How dare I be so critical of someone else's mess when I was sitting in a pile of my own? In addition to this, you can't heal what you never reveal and you can't conquer what you can't confront. The greatest way to overcome obstacles in your life is by facing them head on so that they can be defeated! The power lies in your ability to be honest with the most important person in your life and that person is *you.*

Remember I told you there'd be three principles to abide by throughout this process; **Rules, Reflection & Realness.** Here is your first rule:

Rule #1: Respect Your Process

It's okay to NOT be okay. The worst thing that I've ever done to myself on a difficult day is beat myself up for having a difficult day. It's okay NOT to be okay. It's okay that you woke up feeling out of sorts, and even okay that your affirmation didn't change your mood from deep sadness to immense joy in a matter of seconds. The unrealistic expectation is that you must always be okay. If you're not always okay, then you must have the power to make yourself okay and if you don't have the power to change your entire world in a singular moment, then you are a complete failure...THIS IDEA MUST DIE TODAY!

I used to say that my greatest fear was failure when the reality isn't that I was afraid of failure. I was more afraid of what it would look like to others if I, the coach, the leader, and the motivator, wasn't okay. What if I didn't get everything I wanted from out my business? What if I didn't get everything I wanted out of my personal relationships? What if handling my finances wasn't a breeze? What if pulling up to the gym and not going inside or going inside and being too depressed to work out for longer than 30 minutes was my reality? Would people still love me? Would I be given the same courtesy as someone else who isn't viewed as being in control? Would I still have an opportunity to bounce back and share my success or would I be viewed as a fake who could never overcome all of these things?

With all of these conflicting thoughts and emotions, you know what the wise decision to make was, right? To just act as if I was okay. To pour into clients on days when I didn't think I had a thing to give. To smile at strangers no matter how badly my heart was aching. To seem in control no matter how out of control I felt.

People would respect that. This would gain me the credibility that would make me worthy of success. Right?

In order to receive the best results throughout this journey, you MUST be willing to be honest. No one is watching you. This is your moment to release yourself from the shackles of untruthfulness so that you can soar. This is an opportunity for you to be introduced to parts of yourself that you would have never dreamed belonged to you.

You will experience discomfort as you are stretched to a new level of consciousness. As I write this, I am emotional because witnessing others rise above the very thing that had the potential to destroy them is always an opportunity for me to see myself in someone else. A time to be reminded that I am not the last to rise; there are more people who need to be healed and freed and I am honored that God saw fit for me to be a part of your journey.

Rule #2: Commit!

Keep this guided motivation and meditation somewhere so that you will see it every day and won't be tempted to set it aside until you've completed each day. My number one priority is not to simply get this book into your hands, but for it to become a tool that positively transforms your way of thinking. This will not become another one of your really cute journals that you bought on clearance and only used one page out of it, just to buy another cute one in the same week. I want this to be a tool of effectiveness. Your life will be transformed if you make a decision to commit to your process.

Disclaimer: I am not a therapist. I am a certified coach whose mission is to help you transform your problematic perspectives and implement practical skills that will help you to develop and maintain healthier habits.

Motivate

Day One: Establish Your Truth

There aren't many guarantees in this life, but I know one that is for sure. One guarantee is that every single day you step outside of your home, turn on your TV and even pick up your cell phone, there is something that has the power to influence the way that you feel about yourself. But it only has power if you grant it permission.

Whether positive or negative, it is your responsibility to control the narrative of your life. To begin this journey, it's very important that you identify a foundational truth. This is a word or an affirmation that never changes no matter what happens within your life. You can either create those words for yourself, repeat positive seeds that have been sewn into your life over the years by others, or you can seek out knowledge and truths about yourself in the Bible. Because I believe there was word spoken over your life before you were formed inside your mother's womb, this word should empower you to align your entire life with it, because it will never change. Even when you begin to doubt yourself, even when others doubt you, the words that you share today will be your truth and your foundation.

What are your foundational truths?

_____

_____

_____

You are exposed to so many thoughts and ideas that can influence you into believing lies about yourself, in spite of what your foundational truth tells you. It has always been your responsibility to establish a truth about yourself, but because of the factors that influence you and its power, it's even more important now that you recite them daily, some days even hourly. You decide what you ground yourself in; will you be grounded in love and light or will you be grounded in hatred and darkness? Whatever that is, you must not allow yourself to be swayed by the winds that blow, but rather strong enough to stand firmly and allow the gusts of winds to pass you by like a cool breeze.

What is a truth that you have established about yourself?

_____

_____

These will be your positive affirmations.

List five affirmations and recite them with conviction before you begin each day.

_____

_____

_____

_____

_____

Best Practice: Make sure that your affirmations are not at random but they are specific to your life and your circumstance.

    Example: If you struggle with fear an affirmation could be _"I release all thoughts of fear and believe that I am capable of anything."_

Planting yourself in truths will have such an enormous impact on your life as a professional, regardless of your industry. Whether you're climbing the corporate ladder, building a business from the ground up, leading a ministry or are an entertainer, your power lies in your confidence. Your confidence lies in what you have decide to ground yourself in. Take on today knowing that you are a seed that has been planted and deeply rooted in the words that you have written above.

"These are your truths and the lies of opposition are no match for those words."

~Lanasia Angelina

Which of the three principles will you rely on today?

- **Rules**

- **Realness**

- **Reflection**

How will this principle be of assistance to you? _____

_____

As you go into this day, be motivate

walking word, spoken for goodne

truth in the way that you speak to

others.

Rise & Be Great.

Meditate

Night One: Establish Your Truth

Great Evening,

My prayers today have been for you. As you experience this journey of creating balance within your life, it's so important that you take the proper time to reflect on the thoughts that influence your decisions and the decisions that shape your entire life.

Today, as you began your day with motivation, you centered your thoughts on positive affirmations and foundational truths. My hope is that you recited these words and allowed them to be a guide for your thoughts, emotions and decisions. Recitation helps you to keep your truths at the forefront of your mind, so before you begin reflection this evening, let's go back and reference your truths. Say them aloud and as you speak those words out loud, connect them to an event throughout your day.

1. Which event in your life today is connected to an affirmation that you created this morning?

2. Which affirmation(s) was that?

    _____

3. Did you maintain power and control over your thoughts, emotions and behaviors when this event occurred?

    _____

4. If so, express to yourself in this moment how proud you are to have aligned your actions with the words that you spoke.

    _____

5. If not, identify what hindered you from staying in alignment with the affirmation that you recited this morning.

    _____

6. Were there any doubts associated with the affirmations that you recited today?

    _____

7. If so, list them: _____

8. What characteristics do you possess which prove that your doubt(s) are no match for your truth?

_____

9. Recite your truths again but before each one, breathe deeply, envision yourself already in the place as the person you envision and say "I believe with my whole heart..." (Example: I believe with my whole heart that I am financially free.)

10. Repeat the last step over and over again until you feel it within.

11. Smile and know that without a shadow of a doubt that whatever truth has been spoken about your life before you were born will never change.

"You are already that person. You just have to put yourself in that place."

~Pharrell Williams

Rest & Be Well.

Motivate

Day Two: Prioritization

You didn't think I'd leave a little structure and planning out of a book titled "The Balance Book" completely, now did you? This helps to free up space for you to achieve the "life balance" within your mind.

Each day, you create to-do lists, add things to your digital planners so that you "don't forget", use different color markers, sticky notes and make lines and lines of "things to do" on your hard copy planners. Yet, somehow, only half of what you write down is actually getting accomplished. Saying *half* was me being generous. It's so important that you are handling your business instead of creating busy-ness. By having so much to do, what needs to be done is never completed, completed later than it should be or not completed at the standard that you are capable of achieving. Eliminating the busy-ness will help you get back to your business. It's time for you to create a culture of success within your habits. This way, success will no longer be a thing that you have to chase, but instead it will be drawn to you because it will become your right as a result of your behaviors.

Create an efficient to-do list:

Step 1. Throw out your old one

Step 2. What MUST be done today? (Laundry, groceries, workout, meditation, etc.)

Step 3. What else is to be done today?

Step 4. What MUST to be done this week?

Step 5. What else is to be done this week?

Step 6. Review steps 2-5, then remove at least one thing from each of those lists because everything isn't as important as you believe.

Step 7. Ask yourself: "Is there something that didn't get added to my list that is a priority?" Also, is there anything else on your list that can be handled next week, next month, or maybe even next year?

Step 8. What can you hire someone else to do? Or which tasks do should you ask for help with completing so that you can be effective in another area?

I review my to-do list this exact way every single day because often times, I overwhelm myself with even the thought of everything that I have to do today, tomorrow and for the rest of my life. The main reason why is because it's all usually on one page. How is your plan for studying for a course, starting a new business and planning your next event all going to be accomplished within 24 hours, without even including sleep? It won't! That's why you haven't been able to get anything done.

The principle that you should focus on as you schedule your life and get your priorities in order is ***realness***. I know that you have been told that you can do anything. This statement is true, just know that "anything" doesn't have to all fit into one day. God willing, you'll have a lifetime to manifest every goal that you've taken the initiative to write down and had the courage to dream about, but you are getting your life in order today by simply knowing what comes first. Make sure that your to-do list is **S**pecific, **M**easurable, **A**ttainable, **R**ealistic and **T**imely.

Which of the three principles will you rely on today?

- **Rules**

- **Realness**

- **Reflection**

How will this principle be of assistance to you? _____

_____

Rise & Be Great.

Meditate

Night Two: Prioritization

I struggled with anxiety for years. Lack of prioritization not only affects your ability to accomplish anything - tasks great or small, but it also affects your mood. Not completing my tasks was the root of most of my anxiety. I'd spend my entire day doing everything that wasn't a part of the plan, then toss and turn all night knowing that nothing important was even completed. I was driving myself mad, by choice. It's crazy to think how often you and I have chosen the madness and chaos that exists within our lives. Keep in mind that every time you make a choice to do one thing, it's an equal choice not to do something else. Whether you want to admit it or not, you have in many ways contributed to your own anxiety.

"The biggest regret I've ever had was not showing up for me"

~**My dear friend, Larissa Carlton**

I also take the time to create a schedule for the week, the month and each quarter very specifically. Throw out, without hesitation, everything that makes your life busy but doesn't help you to handle your business.

Rest & Be Well.

Motivate

Day Three: Awareness

Most people think that the worst end of the stick is failure, but failure is not the opposite of success. Failure is not the absence of success. Failure is a necessary part of the journey as you pursue success within every season of your life. The worst that could happen is not that you fail or have a setback; the worst is that you fall short and never reflect on ways to get better.

The worst thing I had ever done in my life was to not be aware of the unprofitable cycles that I was repeating over and over again, never acknowledging how I could use life's roadblocks as stepping stones. That alone makes me want to "Reclaim My Time."

However, being in a state of constant *reflection* forced me to closely observe my own actions, identify the root and make the necessary adjustments that would lead me down a path of success. I had to become intentional about recognizing the shifts in my moods if I wanted to maintain control over them and ultimately, regain control of my life.

Step One:

You have successfully completed day one and two of your guided motivation and meditation. Identify how you feel. Focus on your five senses, one at a time today. Today will be a day of awareness, an awareness of things going on around you, and awareness of the things going on within you.

1. What do you see? _____
    _____

2. What do you hear?_____
    _____

3. What do you feel? _____
    _____

4. What do you smell? _____
    _____

5. What do you taste? _____
    _____

6. What are you thinking right now? _____

_____

7. What are you feeling? _____

_____

8. Are you in a good mood or a bad mood? _____

_____

Now I want you to become aware of why you feel this way. Was there something that you experienced throughout yesterday that made you feel this way? _____

_____

9. Do you feel energized or tired? _____

_____

10. Do you feel motivated or are you struggling to find inspiration today? _____

_____

Step Two:

For any positive thought or emotion that you identified, I want you to breathe slowly, and focus on those thoughts only. Allow them to grow. Water them with attention. Bring every bit of energy towards those thoughts that are good.

If you wrote down anything negative, I want you to identify why you feel this way. Do you have the power to resolve the problem that causes you to feel this way? _____

_____

If not, then repeat this quote by Reinhold Niebuhr:

"God grant me the serenity to accept the things that I cannot change."

"God grant me the courage to change the things that I can."

Here you will strategize a resolution by creating a solution statement. _____

_____

(Example: "I'm in a bad mood because _____but I have the power to change that by…"

Next, repeat these words:

God grant me the wisdom to know the difference between things that I can and cannot change.

If it was out of your control, release the negative feelings into the atmosphere so that whomever has the power to alter this situation may grasp hold of it. If it was within your control, understand that the power you need to change things is already on the inside of you.

Step Three:

Be aware and alert today. Be mindful of the things you say, the music you listen to, the conversations you indulge in and just make mental notes of it all. Remove yourself from toxic situations, and if possible, do so immediately. Be aware of your posture, your language and all things that contribute to your health and wealth. Contrary to what the Instagram fitness model told you, health is holistic and what you feed your spirit is just as, if not more important than, what you feed your body. Feed your spirit with positivity, motivation, and even solitude at times. Be present and invite yourself in to experience real moments.

Which of the three principles will you rely on today?

- **Rules**

- **Realness**

- **Reflection**

How will this principle be of assistance to you? _____

_____

Rise & Be Great.

Meditate

Night Three: Awareness

You will end the night the same way that you began your day. Identify how you feel. Focus on your five senses, one at a time. What might you have become more aware of today that is otherwise overlooked or ignored completely because it's a norm for you? Was it the lyrics of the music that you listened to? Did you find yourself a little uneasy in an otherwise comfortable situation today? How did you feel about yourself today? What thoughts and feelings were you most closely connected to today?

1. What do you see? _____

2. What do you hear? _____

3. What do you feel? _____

4. What do you smell? _____

5. What do you taste? _____

6. What are you thinking right now? _____

_____

7. What are you feeling? _____

8. Are you in a good mood or a bad mood? _____

9. Do you feel energized or tired? _____

10. Do you feel motivated or are you struggling to find inspiration

today? _____

The power of the mind allows you to relive the day with your five senses and alter your perception of it completely. What may have felt like a loss today may have in fact been a lesson. Perception becomes reality and you are only connected to the memory that you recall inside of your mind by way of your interpretation.

How do you want to remember this day? _____

_____

Meditate on the exact thoughts and emotions that this day brought to you and channel that energy into something positive.

What strength did you gain from the weakness you felt? _____

_____

What joy did you experience and why?_____

_____

Meditate on those thoughts. Present your mind with your emotions.

Rest & Be Well.

Motivate

Day Four: Express Gratitude

One grave disservice that you offer to yourself is the worry of tomorrow, as though it will add another day to your life. The only thing that worrying about yesterday and tomorrow does for you is take away the joy of today. In no way am I encouraging that you lay down all responsibilities and live life as a hippie; no judgment of personal choice. But what I am challenging you to do is look around you and appreciate this moment, for this moment is all that truly exists. It's the only thing that you have until it has passed so don't let it pass you by without expressing your sincere gratitude for it.

Before you read any further...Smile! Today is going to be a great day. I'm sure you have your reasons to be sad, upset, disappointed, angry and every other emotion that doesn't breed life but today, be intentional about appreciating the good within your life.

It would be unrealistic for me to encourage you to take good thoughts towards difficult situations because you do not have the power to change every situation in your life right away. A more attainable idea is that you transform the way you perceive the difficulties within your life. This is how you begin to develop a grateful heart within all situations. It's not about pretending to be okay and ignoring how you feel because that goes against our first principle which is "realness". *The goal for this exercise is not for you to see all things as good, but to understand that in everything, it's working for your good.*

The wrong things are falling apart so that the right things can fall together. The 'shaking' is always for the 'making.' The madness is for the molding. This is your reason to be grateful.

Step One: Inhale, Exhale, and Smile.

Step Two: Create a list of situations in your life that you have not been able to see as good._____

Step Three: Read your list out loud.

Step Four: Go back to your list and identify one reason you have to be grateful for this current "difficulty".

Step Five: Repeat these words…I am grateful for (your difficult challenges) because it produce(s) (positive outcome) within my life. (Example: I am grateful for "the breakup" because it gave me time to get to know myself, spend more time with God and identify what I don't want for my next relationship OR I am grateful for my *bills* because paying them keeps a roof over my head.)

Step Six: Express gratitude for the simple things that you take for granted.

Step Seven: Express gratitude for what you _don't_ have.

Step Eight: Express gratitude for the goodness that is being drawn to you now. As you rejoice for your breakthrough, it's being drawn to you. As you rejoice for your victory, it's being drawn to you.

"A grateful heart is the beginning of greatness".

~James E. Faust

Which of the three principles will you rely on today?

-   **Rules**

- **Realness**

- **Reflection**

How will this principle be of assistance to you? _____

_____

Rise & Be Great.

Meditate

Night Four: Express Gratitude

The day may or may not have been everything that you imagined. If it was, bask in that glory and don't feel bad for one moment in the enjoyment of life. Don't think about tomorrow; don't think about yesterday. Enjoy the moment of happiness and fullness. If it wasn't the best day for you, the good news is you can now relax and rid your mind of all of the day's worries. Whether you have a lot on your plate for tomorrow or things that you didn't even accomplish today because your schedule was thrown off track, now is not the time to worry or feel anxious about it. Focus on the good of today and list three things that you have to be grateful for:

1. _____

2. _____

3. _____

Now I want you to list three things that made your day a bit difficult:

1. _____

2. _____

3. _____

Now list how you can find lessons from those moments or how they could have been worse:

1. _____

2. _____

3. _____

Meditate on how grateful you are for today's lessons and blessings. You must be grateful for what you do receive, but also be mindful to be grateful for the things that you didn't receive which like sickness, loss, or financial hardship.

If one of these is your current circumstance, I pray that you find the healing and breakthrough you need. Mourn if you need to. Be still if you need to. Scream if you need to. Release those emotions, the gratitude will flow.

Rest & Be Well.

Motivate

Day Five: Develop Your Response to Life

Urban Meyer, head coach of the Ohio State Buckeyes, explains the retention strategy E+R=O in his book entitled "Leadership". This strategy identifies how the *events* in our lives, which are to some degree outside of your control, in combination with your *response* which is what you, most times should have total control over produces your *outcome* which can be altered with any new combination of the first two.

I want to start by saying that I agree with this strategy and have applied it in several of my coaching sessions with clients and most importantly within my own life experiences. I would like to just add a bit to that. Although the response seems to come after the event has already occurred, I believe that it's extremely important that you in fact, develop your response **before** the event. This way, when you are faced with a situation that seems a little difficult to handle, you are already grounded in what your response to it will be.

A soldier doesn't go into battle and decide to give his/her blood, sweat and tears once opposition has already attacked. The soldier makes a decision when he signs up, when he trains, when he wakes up before the sun every morning, when he puts on his armor, and when he congregates with his brothers. So by the time he gets to the battlefield, his mind is already made up. Whether he is afraid or thinks that he has no chance of coming out alive, his response to give his blood, sweat and tears is already made up, so he does it without hesitation.

This is why you must develop your response first. The obstacles are inevitable; knowing that they're coming gives you the opportunity to develop a mindset that will strengthen you for when it comes.

1. What opposition are you expecting to face today? ____

_____

_____

_____

2.   What will be your response to it? _____

_____

_____

Sometimes the opposition isn't external,

sometimes the opposition is within your mind.

3. What thoughts will possibly arise inside your mind
   that attempt to discourage you from pressing forward?

_____

_____

_____

4. What will your response be to those thoughts and
   feelings? _____

_____

5. Develop a bullet   proof   statement   that   will
   be the response to whatever challenges you face today.
   (Example: "I am a winner"… so when doubt creeps up

inside of your mind, when the days challenges don't quite look like it's adding up to a win for you; declare that you have already won.) _____

_____

_____

6. How are you choosing to respond today? _____

_____

Charles R. Swindoll says "Life is 10% what happens to you and 90% how you respond to it".

~Charles R. Swindoll

Which of the three principles will you rely on today?

- **Rules**

- **Realness**

- **Reflection**

How will this principle be of assistance to you? _____

_____

Rise & Be Great.

Meditate

Night Five: Develop Your Response to Life

Did you encounter a situation where you had to activate your response? _____

If so, what was the outcome? _____

Did the power of the response keep you focused on your goals or did you fall short this time? _____

_____

Consistency is key. I know all too many people with journals that are filled with dozens of affirmations. They have vision boards that have all these powerful affirmations pasted onto them but still struggle to develop and maintain better habits and do what it takes to create a better life.

Why is this? _____

It's because the cost of manifesting these things is just way too high for most. It will cost commitment. It will cost sacrifice. It will cost consistency. It will cost extreme focus.

Recite these words daily, hourly, by the minute until it becomes a part of who you are! Be your own constant reminder of the power that you have inside of you to conquer any of life's challenges.

Recite your response before resting tonight. Meditate on your response in peace and know that your response will become an attitude that produces a positive way of life.

Rest & Be Well.

Motivate

Day Six: Be Intentional

Living day to day without intention and then expecting success is like aiming at a target blindfolded. There's a likelihood that you may hit something, but wouldn't it make more sense to preserve your ammunition? In this case, ammunition being your time, energy and emotions for when you have a clear view of your mark and an execution strategy.

Often times, we confuse being intentional with being in motion. The fact that you are doing does not always mean that it is with focused intent and in any particular direction. The concept of intentionality is defined as "on purpose", but allow me to take a moment to dissect the two definitions of "on purpose":

1. On purpose meaning of cognizant thought.

2. On purpose meaning that I am making decisions that keep me on the path that leads me to fulfilling my assignments on earth.

For this day, I chose the theme *joy*, so no matter what comes my way, whatever setbacks I encounter or disappointments that affect me, I will choose to maintain the spirit of joy. I will surround myself with people who are always spreading joy, while at the same time being the joy for those who aren't necessarily the happiest people today. I will choose music that promotes joy. If I so choose to watch television, I will watch only programs that promote joy. I will feed myself and fill up on the joy that is surrounding me until I become joy with intention.

What's your focus? _____

What's your intention? _____

What's your direction? _____

What will you be intentional about today? Create your narrative(s) of intention.

_____

_____

_____

"Allow your dreams and goals to change, but live an intentional life."

~Kumail Nanjiani

Which of the three principles will you rely on today?

- **Rules**

- **Realness**

- **Reflection**

How will this principle be of assistance to you? _____

_____

Rise & Be Great.

Meditate

Night Six: Be Intentional

Did being intentional make a difference in your day? _____

_____

Meditate on the difference that it made for you. _____

_____

Were you in a better mood? Why or why not? _____

_____

Did you accomplish more things on your checklist today? _____

_____

The things that you involved yourself in, were they "on purpose" according to the two meanings that we discussed during morning motivation? _____

_____

Did your energy attract like energy? Were your thoughts and focus "on purpose"? _____

_____

Do you get where I'm going with this? _____

Studies show that being intentional or doing things ON PURPOSE (the double entendre) increases the likelihood of you achieving your goals in a shorter time frame and achieving higher results.

May your actions be on purpose. (That's a double entendre.)

Rest & Be Well.

Motivate

Day Seven: Cleaning Day Part I

For the next three days, you will be cleaning. Cleaning the clutter out of your life requires more than just a few available hours on a Saturday morning with some Anita Baker playing in the background. The next few days, you will be presented with the opportunity to reflect on what leaves and what remains within your life in regards to ideas, attitudes and behaviors, interpersonal relationships and lifestyle. This cleansing of the mind, body, spirit and essentially, your world, will be vital in your ability to break chains that you allowed to have power over you and truly soar.

The three parts that cleaning day will consist of will be:

Part One: the person

Part Two: the professional

Part Three: your living space

The Person

Realness: Before I was able to change my life, I had to first change my mind. In the process of doing that it was important that I identified three things:

1. The error in my thinking that manifested into destructive decision making.
2. The people who I surrounded myself with daily.
3. The activities that I indulged in.

Thoughts

Today, is the day that you do some cleaning. Identify in depth what thought processes lead to poor decision making habits? Is it thoughts of doubt? A scarcity mindset? Reflect on what you're really experiencing within your mind today and share those thoughts of realness with yourself. No one is here to judge you; no one is here to object to the validity of how you feel right now.

Experience what you're feeling and share those things below.

1. _____

2. _____

3. _____

4. _____

Relationships

I think it's safe to say that many, if not most have experienced involvement with a friend, a romance, a business relationship that was toxic for our growth and development on a personal or professional level at some point in our lives. Because of reasons like history, obligation, our own kindness, and sometimes blood relation, you never sever the tie that is holding you back in so many ways.

Today will be the day that you make a decision! Don't think about it too much, because one thing you do so well is what I like to call "talking ourselves out of a million dollars." This is a term that I adopted to express your ability to create excuses that will grant you the permission to hold onto to things that no longer serve you because of the fear of losing something, someone or an idea that has served as a security blanket and nothing else.

Stop allowing fear to dictate your decisions.

Is there a relationship in your life that's no longer serving you? ___

_____

If so, with whom? _____

Express how: _____

_____

Create a list of what you have to lose by losing them: _____

_____

What risks do you take by keeping them? _____

_____

Identify where you believe that the loss will be greater: _____

_____

Allow that to be what helps you to make that decision. The one is a little more in depth but by the end of this journey, you will know exactly what to do if you have to break a toxic tie.

Habits

You're going to complete a list of the things that you do from day to day. I want you to rank it all from 1-5, with one being the least important, and five being of highest priority.

Are you praying, meditating or spending time alone in deep, relaxing thought while you're still awake every single day, for at least 15 minutes? _____

If not, why? _____

I ask you this because step one of being able to "clean out your life" is by cleansing your mind. Relaxing your mind that fills with more and more clutter each day. I encourage you to create a place for yourself that is dedicated to your daily spiritual cleansing. Dedicate 15 minutes minimum each day to going there, doing a mind dump through journaling, taking slow deep breaths, even lighting a candle and just blocking out all distractions. This is your cleaning place, the place you will go to sort the thoughts that ultimately shape your entire life. How are you expecting a life of cleanliness when your mind is filled with last week's worries, concerns, the music you listened to yesterday, the conversations you had, and the movies you watched? There is no possible way.

EVERYTHING MUST GO!

What have you indulged in this week that must go?

(Example: It can be as 'simple' as watching too much TV to something more complex like indulging in negative and toxic behaviors which could negatively impact your life and the lives of others.)

What have you indulged in this week that can still be done but should be done in moderation? Use the prompts below to get started with your list:

1. (Food)_____

2. (Working) _____

3. (Sleeping) _____

Create your plan of moderation for each one: _____

_____

_____

_____

(Example: I scroll on social media way too much. I will now set a schedule for how many minutes I scroll and the times that I am allowed to. I am not allowed to scroll in the morning before 9 a.m. or at night after 9 p.m. These are the rules that I've set for myself.)

This will help you to increase discipline in your life that will ultimately begin to flow into other areas of weakness that you have.

"Cleanliness makes it easier to see the details."

~Aniekee Tochukwu

Which of the three principles will you rely on today?

- **Rules**

- **Realness**

- **Reflection**

How will this principle be of assistance to you? _____

_____

Rise & Be Great.

Meditate

Night Seven: Cleaning Night Part I

The most difficult part about cleaning day for me had always been identifying what **_needed_** to go and what I **_wanted_** to go. It was very difficult for me to decide after identifying what needed to go, when it should go, but also having to decide in which specific order I needed to begin essentially cleaning things out of my life. It all just required too much effort in thought. So allow me to simplify it for you.

Out of the list of things that you decided should go this morning, which needs the most immediate attention?

Which Thought? _____

Which Person? _____

Which Habit? _____

What are you losing by holding on to this thing?

This thought: _____

This person: _____

This habit: _____

What steps will you commit to going into this week that will help

you to keep this part of your life clean?

    The thought: _____

    The person: _____

    The habit: _____

Imagine your life without:

    The thought: _____

    The person: _____

    The habit: _____

What differences do you see in your life on the other side of…?

    The thought: _____

    The person: _____

    The habit: _____

Meditate on your ability to commit! Refer back to this day as often as needed to remind yourself of where you've been, where you are now and the ability to imagine how far you can go.

Rest & Be Well.

Motivate

Day Eight: Cleaning Day Part II

As I stated before, Cleaning Day is dissected into three parts: the person, the professional, and the living space. I hope that you identified everything that must go as it pertains to your thoughts, the company you keep and the habits in which you indulge. Next, it's time for you to identify the chains you've shackled yourself to within your professional life. What has been holding you back within your career? This exercise will be very similar to the one before, instead your focus and energy will be towards enhancing the professional.

Where are you now within your career? _____

_____

Are you happy within this space? _____

_____

If so, explain why: _____

_____

If not, explain why not: _____

_____

Where do you see yourself five years from now within your career?

_____

Are your thoughts, surroundings and habits leading you to this place? (Refer to Day One.) _____

_____

What specific thoughts are leading you to this place? _____

_____

What specific surroundings (people, environment) are leading you to this place? _____

_____

What specific habits are leading you to this place? _____

_____

Ask yourself the same three questions and replace "are" with "are not".

What specific thoughts are not leading you to this place? _____

_____

What specific surroundings (people, environment) <u>are not</u> leading you to this place? _____

_____

What specific habits <u>are not</u> leading you to this place? _____

_____

Now I want you to identify which thoughts, surroundings and habits look more like your life every day because of the choices you make. Are they the ones that lead you towards the goal or drives you away from the goal? _____

_____

This day, make a commitment to rid your life of the thoughts, surroundings and habits that drive you further away from achieving your goals. ***<u>Success and failure each require a particular degree of commitment.</u>*** The commitment goes far beyond your words. The commitment is in the decisions that you make daily because these are the decisions which ultimately shape your life.

What will you commit to today? Cleanliness or clutter? _____

_____

Which of the three principles will you rely on today?

- **Rules**

- **Realness**

- **Reflection**

How will this principle be of assistance to you? _____

_____

Rise & Be Great.

Meditate

Night Eight: Cleaning Night Part II

I hope that your entire day was lived *on purpose* and that your thoughts, your surroundings and your habits were all in alignment with what you are assigned to fulfill within this season of your life.

For Cleaning Night Part II use this time to reflect on the decisions that you make and the results that they produce.

Three key components that shape your world are your thoughts, your surroundings and your habits. Review this morning's list and ask yourself:

What thoughts were prevalent inside of my mind today? _____

_____

Were those thoughts drawing me nearer or further away from my goals? _____

_____

Who or what did I surround myself with today? _____

_____

Did my surroundings today inspire me to stay on the path towards

my goals? _____

_____

What habits did I allow myself to succumb to today? _____

_____

Will those habits be conducive to my success? _____

_____

Tally up your answers and if the majority were positives that lead
you towards your purpose, stay on that path. Also identify how
you can be stronger in this area where you have already expressed
strength and discipline? Keeping metrics helps you to clearly
identify areas within your life that you are improving, stagnant or
digressing.

If the majority were negatives that drive you further from success,
veer off from that path and get on the right track - QUICK! Identify
the exact things that lead you further from your goal path. Identify
why.

Identify your plan of action to conquer it. _____

_____

Which of the three principles will you rely on today?

- **Rules**

- **Realness**

- **Reflection**

How will this principle be of assistance to you? _____

_____

Rest & Be Well.

Motivate

Day Nine: Cleaning Day Part III

As you continue throughout your journey of creating a healthy balance of applying pressure and sustaining peace, I want you to understand the significance of creating a safe space and protecting yourself from any chaos, particularly in your own home.

Although it may seem as simple as an unfolded sweater and an un-mopped floor, home should be treated as your temple. It's the place where you can go to rid your mind of the clutter, but how can that be achieved if you're surrounded by clutter? I know that with your super busy schedule, the deep cleaning can be pushed back and put off, but I need you to make it a priority this week, starting with making your bed every morning.

This small task will give you a sense of achievement and even lessens stress. "By making your bed, you are starting to declutter your space. A decluttered space lowers your level of stress. You don't waste mental energy.

After your bed has been made, clear the space on your floors in your bedroom of anything that doesn't belong.

Shine your counter tops, night stands, dressers, mirrors.

I understand that this requires time, but the time and energy that you spent on cleaning has just afforded you the opportunity to receive a new level of peace throughout your day. You now have one less thing to worry about, one less thing on your to-do list and before you have even left your home, you have already achieved several things.

Create a list of things to clean throughout the rest of this week, even if just one new thing each day. Commit to decluttering your natural life because it affects the way you function throughout your day as a professional.

What is a small thing that you can commit to cleaning within your home today? _____

Add that to your list of duties, with a specific time. *"The things that get scheduled are the things that get done."* ~Robin Sharma

Cleaning should be prioritized just as everything else is.

What is your biggest cleaning task? _____

Add that to your list of duties with a specific date and time.

When I speak about motivation, more comes to mind than what you are trying to attain as the professional. I want the person to be motivated within every level of their lives because who you are within your personal life directly affects the way that you perform within your professional life; oftentimes when you least expect it. The best way to prepare yourself to handle the challenges that will present themselves is to take care of home. This gives you the energy to tackle life's challenges knowing that you have a safe space awaiting you each day, a clean space and serene space. You must value your home as a metaphor for how you value your life.

Be motivated today in knowing that you have started your day on a high note and home is your safe space.

Which of the three principles will you rely on today?

- **Rules**

- **Realness**

- **Reflection**

How will this principle be of assistance to you? _____

_____

Rise & Be Great.

Meditate

Night Nine: Cleaning Night Part III

I'm extremely excited about what you have accomplished so far throughout this journey. You've remained committed to the process. That's something to be proud of! Just a heads up, I'm about to put a damper on your already long day with two fun facts.

#1 Businesses Fail

The Small Business Association (SBA) states that only 30% of new businesses fail during the first two years of being open, 50% during the first five years and 66% during the first 10.[2]

I know you're probably thinking, "Why is this information significant and how on earth does it tie into 'Cleaning Day'?" I'm so glad that you asked.

Businesses fail for a number of reasons; the reasons that apply today are perseverance and commitment. My goal for this book is for it to become a tool that you can lean on in a time of need, but in order to identify the true value throughout this journey is to remain committed. That not only applies to this journey, but let that be a mantra throughout your life. Commitment will be your most powerful weapon as you continue on the path of great achievement. Start by re-committing to your cleaning today.

Remember those "small" commitments and "small" achievements each day are what add up to success. Commit to it.

#2 Relationships Fail

Once a relationship lasts a year, the likelihood that it ends begins to drop precipitously. Over the first five years, the rate falls by roughly 10 percentage points each year, reaching about 20 percent for both straight and gay couples.

Again, how does this apply to today's theme of "Cleaning Day"? I'm so glad that you asked.

Think about the first time or even the last time that you fell in love. You were ever so passionate. You felt like your soul was on fire, but in a good way. All you could think about was this love and you were so excited to experience this love, but then the love became old and played out. It was no big deal to be there anymore and before you knew it, you were just "going through the motions". No passion, no excitement, no progress... just movement. Appreciation was no longer a concept that either party could relate to and fun was a foreign language.

As you clean today, imagine the way that love felt, what about it inspired you? Did that love make you want to become a better version of yourself? Imagine as you clean that you are again experiencing that high feeling of love but with newer memories.

Enjoy cleaning.

Repeat these words: "*It is a pleasure and an honor to clean the space that I call home and relax in the thought of knowing that 'I'm on my way'*.

Committing to this cleaning with great passion is just one less achievement that I have to worry about that lies before me."

I know I just made cleaning extremely deep, right? But...if you are not extreme then mediocrity is just waiting for you around the block. This may be a little intense but your future is worth it. *The success of your future requires your intensity.*

Rest & Be Well.

Motivate

Day Ten: Be Anxious for Nothing - Worry Free Day

Philippians 4:6-8 NKJV *Be anxious for nothing, but in everything by prayer and supplication, with thanksgiving, let your requests be made to God. And the peace of God, which passes all understanding will guard your hearts and minds through Christ Jesus.*

Matthew 6:25-27 NIV *Therefore I tell you, do not worry about your life, what you will eat or drink or about your body, what you will wear. It is not life more than food, and the body more than clothes? Look at the birds of the air, they do not sow or reap or store away in barns, and yet your heavenly father feeds them. Are you not much more valuable than they? Can any one of you by worrying add a single hour to your life?*

Do you have worries today? Is it regarding your family, your career, or your health? _____

_____

_____

Today, I am worried about _____

_____

_____

Fortunately, I am worry free today, but I will consider a frequent

worry to guide me for future reference.

Ask yourself these questions:

   1. What is the worst that could happen? _____

   _____

   2. What is the likelihood of the outcome that I worry about

   coming to pass? _____

   3. If the worst case scenario were to come to pass, what would

   be my ideal response to it? _____

   _____

   4. Am I capable of responding in an ideal way to this situation?

   _____

   5. If I am not capable of responding in an ideal way, why not?

   _____

6. What strengths do I have that could assist me in responding ideally? _____

_____

7. If the ideal response is an unlikely one, what response to the situation that I am capable of utilizing will give me the most profitable outcome? _____

_____

_____

8. Next, it's important to focus on the most profitable outcome and the response that will result in it all day long.

Now that you have changed the direction of your thoughts from worry and stress to relaxation and relief, you are ready to focus on all of the days tasks that will help you take one step further in the direction of achieving a new level of success.

Which of the three principles will you rely on today?

- **Rules**

- **Realness**

- **Reflection**

How will this principle be of assistance to you? _____

_____

Rise & Be Great.

Meditate

Night Ten: Be Anxious For Nothing - Worry Free Day

Before you read any further today, take a minute to breathe deeply.

Inhale.

Exhale.

Repeat these words. "Everything that I need is already within me. I am in total control." Anything that happens in my life is not happening to me, but instead it's happening for me. Answer the questions below and identify how all good things are working for you.

Did your worst case scenario happen today? _____

_____

If so, how did you respond? _____

_____

If not, aren't you glad that you didn't spend your day worrying about it? _____

Meditate on these thoughts.

You have the power to change the narrative for your life.

Rest & Be Well.

Motivate

Day Eleven: Create a Strength & Weakness Combination

There is a huge misconception that your strengths will always be your strengths and that your weaknesses will always remain your weaknesses. I ask you to challenge that notion and expand your mind to the idea that all things have the potential to change. Without intention, strengths can easily become weaknesses and with intention, weaknesses can either be staffed or strengthened. This is why acknowledging what your strengths and weaknesses or opportunities are is important. Knowing this will enable you to develop what I like to call a "perfect pair." Allow me to explain:

Math has never been one of my particular strengths. I have failed many complicated math courses but knowing that I have a strength in developing relationships and leveraging my network allows me to staff the help that I need in that specific area. Identifying this as my weakness also gives me the opportunity to educate myself and set aside time to learn how to complete tasks that require complicated math.

Review your agenda today and create a list of three strengths that will assist you in accomplishing things on that agenda.

Strengths

1. _____

2. _____

3. _____

Now, I encourage you to list three weaknesses that may hinder you from completing that agenda.

Weaknesses

1. _____

2. _____

3. _____

Now I want you to find and pair the perfect strength that you will utilize in the event that your weakness interferes with you accomplishing today's agenda. Lean on this strength throughout your day. *Know that even in a time of weakness, there is something inside of you that has the power to solve the problems you may face.*

Which of the three principles will you rely on today?

- Rules

- Realness

- Reflection

How will this principle be of assistance to you? _____

_____

Rise & Be Great.

Meditate

Night Eleven: Strength! Strength! No Weaknesses

Another strength that I have depended upon greatly has been my ability to reflect. Reflection has allowed me to focus on identifying my weaknesses. This enables me to go even deeper to understand two things "why I identify these areas as weaknesses?" and "how I can implement effective practices in to my life that will help me to transform them into strengths?"

Reflect on the weaknesses that you allowed to be a limitation within your today, if any, and ask:

What makes this a weakness for you? _____

_____

What are some effective strategies that you can implement that will assist you in strengthening this particular area? _____

_____

How frequently will you implement these strategies? _____

_____

Visualize yourself conquering this weakness and living a life where you're no longer bound.

Rest & Be Well.

Motivate

Day Twelve: Discipline

Discipline was often one of those concepts that I just couldn't quite conquer. Doing what needs to be done even when I don't feel like it? Like, who came up with that idea? Now for some things, like loving my friends even when they're un-loveable, you know the way that God loves you when you're out of line? Yea, that way; that's discipline that requires no effort, but for other things, like going to the gym seven days a week before the sun comes up, was more like a complex math problem that I just couldn't seem to find the solution for. I could not seem to wrap my mind around the idea of going, even after lying in bed, comparing the pros and cons (there were always more pros stacked up against my one con which was typically that my bed was comfortable). Somehow, even after visualizing the six pack that I always dreamed about and had the ability to acquire, I still couldn't move from that sinful mattress. It was never the comfort that I rested in physically that kept me in that bed. It was the comfortable subpar mindset that I had developed and grown attached to that needed to be addressed. *I didn't need to change my mattress; I needed to shift my mindset.*

What area of your daily routine do you find you are the least disciplined in? _____

Why? _____

Now let's compare the pros and cons...

What will you lose by doing this thing? _____

_____

What will you gain by doing this thing? _____

_____

What is your greatest barrier when it comes to doing this thing? __

_____

Why? _____

How can you be proactive in conquering this barrier?

1. _____

2. _____

3. _____

As you take on your day, prepare to follow through. Prepare to rise above the thoughts that have kept you stagnant in any particular area of your life. Mediocrity requires little to no effort towards discipline. If greatness is the goal then don't just dream it, make it your reality by fighting against the enemies of comfort and fear of change.

"Discipline is the bridge between goals and accomplishments."

~Jim Rohn

Which of the three principles will you rely on today?

- **Rules**

- **Realness**

- **Reflection**

How will this principle be of assistance to you? _____

_____

Rise & Be Great.

Meditate

Night Twelve: Discipline

First, take this time to reflect again on the area(s) where you lack the most discipline.

Reflection brings you back to square one and centers your focus back to the aspect of your life that needs the attention in this current moment. Before you beat yourself up for "falling" or jump for joy for "rising", envision yourself on the other side of consistent discipline. Imagine the results that the sacrifice now will bring you later. This is your *why*. This is why you must make a decision in this moment to commit to yourself whether your decisions today lead you to "rise" or to "fall". Before you ask me "why do I need to commit? I did well today", always keep this saying in mind that I like to use every time I feel like I've done enough.

"Today's paycheck won't cover tomorrow's bill."

~Lanasia Angelina

Yes, you did well and you deserve to rejoice in your ability to remain diligent, but the process continues and tomorrow you must recommit to stay the course.

Did the opportunity present itself for you to express discipline in the area that you mentioned earlier today? _____

How did you handle it? Did your decisions draw you closer to or further away from your results? _____

_____

Which specific decisions drew your closer? _____

_____

Which specific decisions pulled you further away? _____

_____

Now, I will leave you with this question: Was the moment of satisfaction worth your results? _____

_____

If the answer is no, recommit yourself today by reciting this mantra.

"My future is worth the sacrifice today. My (insert result) is worth me sacrificing (insert sacrifice) today."

Rest & Be Well.

Motivate

Day Thirteen: DREAM BIG!

If the dream doesn't scare you, then you're not dreaming big enough!

Or maybe you're just in disbelief that you're much more amazing than you could have ever imagined. You could be afraid of the impact that your greatness will have on the hearts, minds and essentially the world! Let's just go with the latter.

You will not settle for thoughts that match your capabilities. You will have the courage today to dream bigger than you ever have before. To imagine that the house, the car, the career, the marriage, the friendships and the future that you envisioned belongs to you! Imagine that everything that has been a burden to you and for you is lifted! Imagine that you are spiritually free! Mentally free! Financially free! Dream bigger than you have ever imagined because God has the ability to do exceedingly and abundantly above all that you could ever ask think or imagine (Ephesians 3:20).

Your ways are not His ways! Your thoughts are not His thoughts (Isaiah 55:8)! Dream enormous today!

As I'm writing this today, I'm excited for you! This is heartfelt, organic motivation. I know that you sometimes feel like you have the burdens of the world on your shoulder and the idea of imagining beyond your circumstance seems almost impossible, but today is not like any other day! Imagine greatness because if you can see it, then it's yours! Recite that it belongs to you. We'll keep today short and sweet.

What will you dare to dream big about today? _____

_____

Focus on that singular thought with enthusiasm. The energy you exude will be drawn back to you.

Which of the three principles will you rely on today?

- **Rules**

- **Realness**

- **Reflection**

How will this principle be of assistance to you? _____

_____

"So many of our dreams seem impossible, then they seem improbable, and then, we summon the will, they soon become inevitable."

~Christopher Reeve

Rise & Be Great.

Meditate

Night Thirteen: DREAM BIG!

Whoever said you couldn't dream with your eyes opened was lying. I'm probably more excited than you are about reflecting on the day. I hope that you envisioned your dreams with the belief that they will come true. You have the power to manifest whatever ideas that you create inside of your mind. Why not create ideas that are consistent with the life that you want to have.

So tell me, what did you dream about today? _____

_____

When you imagined this dream what feelings were associated with

it? _____

_____

If they were good feelings, share why... _____

_____

If they were bad feelings, share why... _____

_____

It's important that you are **real** with yourself about why you are excited or discouraged when you imagine your big dreams. Awareness was an earlier theme that you experienced throughout this journey. It's so imperative that you are aware of the feelings that you associate with your big ideas. That specific energy and path of beliefs can lead you either closer towards connecting to your dreams or draw you further away.

I also want you to rely on the principle of realness today but in this way:

Are your big dreams even **real**istic? What I mean when I say that is, are they attainable? Are they measurable? This will help you identify where some of the doubt, if any, comes from.

Next, ask yourself again: Are my dreams even **real**? Is this a dream that I want for myself or am I trying to acquire this dream for validation? Am I trying to acquire this dream from appreciation? Am I trying to accomplish this dream to prove someone else wrong?

Make the dream about you and about purpose then take everyone else out of the equation.

What about you, with no other factors included, makes you want this dream? _____

_____

What about your purpose makes you want to manifest this dream?

_____

Meditate on those two answers and either alter the dream to align it with the plan or alter the plan to align it with the dream. Either way, something has to give. What will that be? _____

_____

"Dream big but not without probable cause." ~*Lanasia Angelina*

Rest & Be Well.

Motivate

Day Fourteen: Become Something Wonderful!

The most pressing question in life is not "What do I need to do" but rather "What do I need to become?" ~Lanasia Angelina

I used to believe that life was more about doing than becoming. What I mean by that is I was working harder to *do* successful work instead of *becoming* a successful individual. I wasn't creating a culture of success that would allow me to succeed in my work. I was overextending myself in the midst of the deeds and exhausting all of my time, money and energy on something that would never succeed if I didn't do the work necessary to become the person who was ready to receive it all. Success attracts success. As I became love, I attracted love. As I became peace, I attracted peace.

What you need to attract most is what you should focus on becoming the most. Choose one thing to focus on becoming today. Simplifying the process will help you to maximize all of your energy on that specific area of improvement and ultimately stretch you in that direction.

Today, when your mind inevitably contradicts what you have committed your day to focus on becoming, I challenge you to actively redirect your focus with these seven steps:

1. **Acknowledge** - Identify which attitude, thought or emotion you shifted your focus to and what from.

2. **Breathe** - Release any tension from your body so that you may complete this next step in peace.

3. **Smile** - When a smile flashes across your face; dopamine, endorphins and serotonin are all released into your bloodstream, making not only your body relax but also work to lower your heart rate and blood pressure. [4]

4. **Envision** - Imagination directly affects your decision making. If you are imagining with fear, then it will cause you to reluctantly respond situations. However, if your imagination is aligned with courage and hope, then you will trust that any decisions made will benefit your wellbeing.

5. **Speak** – Re-affirm those thoughts to which you have committed.

6. **Focus** – Redirect your focus back to what you have committed to focusing on becoming today.

7. Repeat as often as needed throughout your day.

Which of the three principles will you rely on today?

- **Rules**

- **Realness**

- **Reflection**

How will this principle be of assistance to you? _____

_____

Rise & Be Great.

Meditate

Night Fourteen: Become Something Wonderful

What have you become? _____

Becoming is a process within itself and everyday matters; every moment counts. Every decision affects your being. Every seed of thought that you plant, will determine your manifestations in your season of harvest.

What seeds did you plant today within your imagination? _____

_____

List them: _____

_____

What seeds of action did you sow into the ground today? _____

_____

Will the seeds that you planted ever bear the fruit that you desire? The savory taste of success, the fulfilling taste of love, the crisp taste of joy and peace they require the proper seeds in order to grow.

(Example: Ideas of self-doubt, worry, jealousy and fear will never produce self-confidence, peace, collaboration and courage.)

Regardless of the seeds you planted today, whether in imagination or decision making, the good news is that there is still more ground to cover and you are blessed enough to have more seed left.

What will you do with it? _____

Imagine that you are a seed. Label your seed as the harvest that you want to see manifest.

Harvest -I want to have healthy relationships and a thriving business.

Seed – I will cultivate a space for honesty and support. I will be consistent in my efforts and improve my skillset daily by doing "xyz."

Water that seed with the thoughts that the fruit already belongs to you and instead of waiting patiently for your season of harvest, rejoice in the expectation of its arrival. Doing is not where the success comes from, becoming is.

Meditate with the confidence that you are already that person, you just haven't yet arrived in that place.

Rest & Be Well.

Motivate

Day Fifteen: Two Steps forward. No steps back!

Don't turn around! Don't look back! It's going to seem so close and you're going to be tempted to go there!

Contrary to the rear view mirror that warns that *objects are closer than they appear*, the objects in your rear view are out of your reach. That's not because it's farther in time and distance or further in understanding, but because the person that you are becoming and the goals you are working to achieve are more profitable than everything that is behind you. Do you want to take the long way by turning around and going back or do you want to stay the course, keep moving forward and bring yourself one step closer towards your destiny? _____

Create a list of three temptations that should be behind you that could threaten your potential growth? _____

_____

_____

Why are each of these things so enticing? _____

_____

What are three internal barriers that prevent you from moving

forward? (Example: ideas, emotions, behaviors, life experiences)

_____

_____

What's the worst that could happen if you took a step to get past

these mental blocks? _____

_____

What's the worst that could happen if you went back? _____

_____

Your future is expensive. What I mean by that is it's going to cost

you some things. The price that you will have to pay for your future

will be some of the things from your past. Think about

your experiences as currency. Every time you make a decision that

takes you back, even if just for a moment, you lose some

of the currency that affords your future. Every time your thoughts

and decisions align with the direction that you're headed in, you're

able to pay the toll for the next level in your life.

Are those temptations worth your future? I like to speak life over my finances daily, instead of saying "I can't afford it". I am intentional by saying that it's not in my budget right now. When it comes to making decisions that look enticing for the moment, I spend the currency I need to spend in order to unlock the next level in my life. I have no hesitation with saying "I CAN'T AFFORD IT. I can't afford to turn back! I've come too far to turn back now". I need you to keep these words in mind when you even consider spending your *"cash"* (time, energy, and emotions) on things that no longer serve you.

"I CAN'T AFFORD IT!"

Which of the three principles will you rely on today?

- **Rules**

- **Realness**

- **Reflection**

How will this principle be of assistance to you? _____

_____

Rise & Be Great.

Meditate

Night Fifteen: Two Steps Forward

Can you believe that you're two thirds of the way through this journey? Before you and I get into this evening's meditation, I need you to declare these words: "My future is too expensive; therefore, I can't afford to return back to things that no longer serve me."

I want you to use this time of meditation to REFLECT on the enticing behaviors and attitudes that no longer serve you, but the comfort which makes it appealing to you.

Did you succumb to these thoughts, emotions or behaviors today?

_____

How do you feel knowing that you were strong enough to conquer your temporary desires? _____

OR

How do you feel knowing that you were succumb by the thoughts, emotions or behaviors that you know your future can't afford? ____

_____

Think about your decisions as though it's that time you spent all of your money on impulsive buys and then you couldn't foot the bill for something that you really wanted or needed. I'm going to go out on the limb here and say with great confidence that you probably promised yourself in that moment "this is the last time"…that is until you swiped your card to yet again serve your temporary desires, neglecting the discipline required to afford you what you truly want at a later date and often times even need.

Yes, it's a simpler decision to fulfill your fleeting desires now than it is to be patient for a greater reward, but the cycle will never end until you make a decision in your mind that scratching that itch now will never satisfy you in the way that patience and perseverance will.

Meditate on the fact that now is not worth your later! YOU CANNOT AFFORD IT!

Rest & Be Well.

Day Sixteen: **You Will Win or Learn, But You Will Never Lose**

The best decision I ever made was to transform my perspective towards loss. This is not to say that I am romanticizing the idea of loss or even ignoring the fact that some things go. I am simply acknowledging the power that I have to decide how a shift within my perspective can have a positive impact on how I experience loss.

Is the glass half empty or half full? _____

If it is half empty, then the value is in the fact that I still have room for more. If it's half full then that means that I'm halfway to the finish line and that I've done my due diligence to get this far. I never devalue the work that has brought me to this point.

Today, I want you to declare that the power of perspective will either help you to see the light at the end of the tunnel, challenge you to acquire a new skill or develop the skills that you already possess. Why is this needed? The power of perspective is to get you closer to the light that exists, even though you may not be able to see it right now.

Encourage yourself and make a decision to respond to life as a victor today. Be open to learn from "setbacks and difficulties" and celebrate your wins no matter how small they seem.

Identify a situation where you could potentially lose today:

_____

_____

Will you win over that situation or learn?

_____

_____

Create a winning mantra that you will use daily.

_____

_____

"I never lose. I either win or I learn."

~Nelson Mandela

Which of the three principles will you rely on today?

- **Rules**

- **Realness**

- **Reflection**

How will this principle be of assistance to you? _____

_____

Rise & Be Great.

Meditate

Night Sixteen: Win or Learn – Never Lose

"Losers find excuses to lose. Winners find opportunities to win."

~Lanasia Angelina

The main purpose for this day was for you to understand that all things are working together for your good. If you can just take the time to see it all working around you on your behalf right now, then I promise that it will get you closer to the "finish line" faster.

Finish line is in quotations because there is no finish line…at least not the one that you're imagining. The finish line is where you end when God calls you to be home with Him. Will you have lived your entire life believing that you never accomplished your "ultimate goal"? _____

What if you imagined and appreciated all of the good that this moment brings? So much so that if you were to die today, you can say that you were finished, you're done and that your job is complete? _____

Having this mindset will assist you most in seeing how your "loss" was in fact something working for your good. Where you are now may not be what you imagined, but it's better because you were able to find all of the value the moments that preceded it. The moments that have been gifted to you. These are the wins or the "lessons". Win or learn; never lose!

Did you encounter a situation today where you chose to lose instead of learn? Talk about it.

Since you didn't win in that moment, you have the opportunity to learn now.

So what did you learn from that situation? _____

_____

About life? _____

About yourself? _____

Did you encounter a situation that you chose to win? Talk about it.

_____

_____

Since you were victorious in that situation, how could you apply it in the area that you had to learn today? _____

_____

_____

Imagine yourself responding as the improved version of yourself.

Breathe slowly.

Repeat these words three times:

"All things are working for my good because God is intentional."

Rest & Be Great.

Motivate

Day Seventeen: **You Are Worthy**

I used to measure my self-worth by my accomplishments. There was a point in my life, in which I didn't feel like I had accomplished anything of value and so I deemed myself worthless.

I used to declare my worthiness and then right after wasting the energy to affirm something that I was not align my actions with, I'd follow it up by doing exactly the opposite of what worthiness would entail as far as my behavior goes. I was eating food that was contradictory of my worthiness and having relationships with people who didn't see my worth or value and treated me accordingly. I was backing down from business opportunities and seats at tables that I thought I wasn't good enough for, all because I was lying to myself.

"Worthiness is as worthiness does; worthiness is not as worthiness declares."

~Lanasia Angelina

The decisions that I was making on a daily basis were not aligning with my affirmations of worthiness. I desperately needed to figure out how could I turn this around? How could I change my behaviors to prove that what I was saying was in fact truth and not a lie?

Three steps were required in order to make a change:

1. Raise my **awareness** to my unprofitable thoughts, feelings and behaviors.

2. **Acknowledge** that it needed to change, who was responsible for changing it and how.

3. Develop a plan of **action** for change and execute.

Are you aware of your unprofitable cycles? If so, what are they? List them below. _____

_____

Acknowledge the areas where you have been lying to yourself most with regards to your worthiness.

Create a list of the lies (things that you have declared but not followed through with) that you have, with confidence said to yourself.

_____

_____

How will you? Explain how you will express how worthy you are in your decision-making. Create a list. _____

_____

List everything you have gained by lying to yourself and to others:

_____

_____

Your actions determine how you truly feel about yourself.

List at least five truths that prove how you've truly been feeling about yourself (good or bad). _____

_____

_____

_____

_____

How will you turn those lies into truths? _____

_____

Be Specific: _____

_____

What is the measurable aspect? How will you recognize and record the change? _____

_____

Will the life you live and the resources you have access to help to attain a lifestyle of a new truth? _____

_____

Are you being realistic? Are the chances of success high?

_____

In what time frame will you review the measurable aspect that will determine whether or not you have been successful at altering your lifestyle in this aspect? _____

_____

"Our life is a summation of all of the decisions that we have made as a direct result of how we view and feel about ourselves."

~Lanasia Angelina

Life is what you make it. What are you making your life?

Which of the three principles will you rely on today?

- **Rules**

- **Realness**

- **Reflection**

How will this principle be of assistance to you? _____

_____

Rise & Be Great.

Meditate

Night Seventeen: You are Worthy

Before you begin tonight's meditation I want you to follow these steps:

1. Close your eyes

2. Breathe (inhale and exhale slowly)

3. Relax your muscles

4. Breathe

5. Smile

Regardless of the decisions you made today, I have really good news for you. It's not over. It's not the end. Your life still has purpose. You are still worthy of the win. Your worthiness does not begin and end with a simple decision.

In fact, if you never made another decision today, you would still be worthy. Decisions don't define your value, they determine your outcomes.

As long as there is still breath in your body, you can still prove that you're capable of exuding the greatness that is within you, and proving your worth by making worthy decisions the next time. Now, don't make the mistake of always relying on "next time". Understand that God's love is endless and that your life is proof of your value. Wouldn't it make you feel proud to know that you treated the gift of life as such? _____

Think of a situation you encountered today where you didn't make a decision of worthiness: _____

_____

Why? _____

_____

How did that make you feel? How will that decision impact your life or simply just tomorrow? _____

_____

Create a mantra for that moment that you will keep as ammunition for the next time you need to go to battle with this situation. _____

_____

_____

Think of a situation that you encountered today where you were able to make a decision of worthiness: _____

_____

What made you choose a worthy decision? _____

_____

How did that make you feel? _____

_____

Celebrate that moment. Bring the feeling of pride and gratitude closer to you so that it reminds you for the next time of the feeling of victory that you want to feel instead of the feeling of defeat.

Breathe...smile...you're victorious. All of your decisions are lining up with the path that will ultimately lead you to your destiny.

Rest & Be Well.

Motivate

Day Eighteen: Forgiveness

Forgiveness for a long time had been one of those concepts for me that I just couldn't wrap my mind around. Since I'm being honest, it was one of those concepts that I just *wouldn't* wrap my mind around. At some point in my life, I was influenced to believe that if I had extended forgiveness that I was then accepting an offense or even worse, doing a favor for whomever had offended me.

This forgiveness was not only difficult when it came to its reach being extended to someone else, but I found it to be an even more difficult a task to reach within and forgive myself. It's one thing when someone else sins against you because you know that you had no control over their actions, but how on earth do you forgive yourself when you're supposed to be the main one in life who cares for you and loves you like no one else?

The thought of forgiveness became a burden, but an even heavier burden was the un-forgiveness that I held tightly in my grip, without any plans of letting go. Holding it in my hand was essentially what kept me from the happiness, joy and love that I so desperately needed. Un-forgiveness was all because I made a decision to carry someone else's worst with me while I was at my best. Not even just someone else's, but I was also holding on to my own personal shortcomings. The person that I used to be was holding me back from the destiny that those character building moments were supposed to propel me closer towards. Instead that person became a weight that kept me bound. So how was I supposed to release these shackles? What were the practical steps I needed to implement into my life that would allow me to soar above un-forgiveness? _____

_____

Forgiveness is a process and some things may take more time to forgive than others. The first step to recovery is admitting and I want you to be one step closer to the freedom of forgiveness before you leave your house today.

Acknowledge - Who haven't you forgiven? Why? How is holding onto un-forgiveness helping you? How is holding on to un-forgiveness hurting you? _____

_____

_____

Write down the name(s) of the people whom you haven't forgiven. After their names, write and free yourself with a mantra of forgiveness. (Example: "I forgive _____ for not believing in me.")

_____

_____

I understand that it may take more than a singular moment for your heart to catch up to your words. The more you speak it, the easier it becomes for you to believe it, feel it and live a life free of unforgiveness. Say it every day if you need to. Say it to that person if it helps, but just say it.

What have you not forgiven yourself for? _____

Why? _____

How is holding onto this helping you? _____

_____

How is holding onto this hurting you? _____

_____

Accept - Accept the fact that whatever someone else did to you was outside of your control, so there is no way that you can control it or change the pass by holding onto the offense.

Accept the fact that the parts of yourself that you have yet to forgive is the person that you used to be. Is there something in your power that you can do today, or anytime in the future, to help a situation that you haven't forgiven yourself for? _____

_____

If so, what is within your power to do? _____

_____

What is not within your power to do? _____

_____

I challenge you to release all that is outside of your sphere of altering and commit to what you have the power to change.

Understand that the outcome or response is also outside of your control, even if you so choose to right a wrong.

Practice - Repeat this mantra daily *"I will not carry anyone's worst with me while I am at my best, not even my own. My heart is free from the shackles of un-forgiveness"*

Which of the three principles will you rely on today?

- **Rules**

- **Realness**

- **Reflection**

How will this principle be of assistance to you? _____

_____

Rise & Be Great.

Meditate

Night Eighteen: Forgiveness

In no way did I make the decision to make Day 17 seem as if the process of forgiveness is short, sweet and to the point. I understand that the source of so much of our un-forgiveness is deeply rooted. So, I want to start this evening by saying that your pain matters. Your disappointment matters. Your thoughts, feelings and ideas matter. I would never want to ignore the things that have offended you. I would never want to encourage the idea that you should minimize the experiences that you feel have shaped you or impacted your life in a negative way.

This day, I want you to lean upon the principle of **reflection**. Instead of reflecting on what changed you and why, identify how addressing those feelings made you feel today.

If I made you bring a thought to your pre-frontal cortex that you had buried, then I sincerely apologize. I apologize but at the same time I send you congratulations for being so courageous. Yes, in the beginning it hurts but in the end, you'll be glad that you did it.

That's what forgiveness is, ripping of the bandage to allow the scab to heal.

What were you challenged to rip the bandage off of today? _____

_____

How did that affect your day? _____

_____

Did thinking about it empower you or was it still a sensitive thought for you? _____

_____

Are you ready to commit to the process that forgiveness requires?

_____

How did you respond to that thought as you became aware of it?

_____

A posture of gratitude is so important as you journey your path of forgiveness. It will allow you to connect the dots from the time of the offense to where you are now.

Some people may think "my life would have been better if it had not been for that offense." But are you so sure of that? _____

_____

The power is in your perspective.

Who's to say that if that thing didn't happen to you that you'd still have the blessing of life? That thing could be the very reason that you lived and now you have the privilege of impacting the life of someone else - either through your testimony or your acts of service. Isn't that amazing?

Un-forgiveness is truly a burden that no living man/woman should bear.

"Release that heavy load of un-forgiveness. You deserve to set yourself free."~Lanasia Angelina

Rest & Sleep Well.

Motivate

Day Nineteen: You Are Not an Imposter

For so long, whenever people would tell me how much I inspired or motivated them, instead of enjoying and appreciating their admiration for me, instead I felt ashamed that I wasn't nearly as amazing as they thought I was. I was so busy comparing myself to others who had "better" businesses, "better" speaking abilities, or "better" educational backgrounds than mine, forgetting the fact that I was created in the likeness and image of God. I had the audacity to believe that where I was in my process was beneath me. I thought that would be the sole reason why I wouldn't have the strength, character and ability to be the person who everyone else had already seen. *I had to come to a harsh reality that I was in fact real. I am great!* I am a phenomenal business woman! I am an exceptional speaker and even in acknowledging that I still had opportunities for growth, it was unfair for me to shame my own journey when other people actually developed a love and respect for it.

Now on the contrary, if you're promoting a life that you aren't actually living, then you should ask yourself where your validation comes from.

Why do you feel the need to promote a life that isn't real? _____

_____

What do you gain? _____

What do you lose? _____

If you are living a life that's consistent with the one that you are promoting, ask yourself "why does this make me feel like an imposter?" _____

_____

What qualities do I have that prove that I am not?

1. _____

2. _____

How can I maximize those qualities and focus on them today?

1. _____

2. _____

Today, create a mantra for how bomb, how dope, how amazing, how relentless, and how powerful you are. Play that over in your head like your favorite record over a dope beat that is the sound of your strut allll dayyyy long.

Which of the three principles will you rely on today?

- **Rules**

- **Realness**

- **Reflection**

How will this principle be of assistance to you? _____

_____

Rise & Be Great.

176

Meditate

Night Nineteen: You Are Not an Imposter

The first thing I want you to say to yourself this evening is. "I am killing it! I am phenomenal! I have the power to do amazing things! My effort is enough as long as I know that I've given my best then I have nothing to be ashamed of. I am so proud of me. I am killing it!

So imagine I'm there with you and I want you to brag on yourself a little today. Tell me just how bomb you are: _____

_____

What are your thoughts about yourself today? _____

_____

Do you feel good enough? _____

_____

If so, why? _____

If not, why not? _____

Do you feel like you have put forth an honest version of yourself today? _____

_____

If you haven't, identify when… _____

Why do you think that is…? _____

_____

What did you gain from presenting an embellished version? _____

_____

What is the true version of you that you didn't feel was good enough? _____

_____

What would you have gained by being your truthful self? _____

_____

Do you feel good enough? _____

Why or why not? _____

_____

List things about yourself that prove your worth… I'll start:

   1. You were created in God's image and His likeness.

Your turn…take your time and say these things out loud as you write them down. Inhale and exhale in between.

_____

_____

I understand that sometimes you don't see the results that you expected to come from the work that you put in. With everyone on social media telling you how proud they are and with your family looking to you as a savior, you feel like you can do better. But I'm going to ask you one more time - did you do your best today? ____

_____

If so, be proud of that.

If not, the fact that you're acknowledging it now will work wonders for your tomorrow.

What can you do better tomorrow? _____

_____

Envision yourself in that place, doing that thing! You're killing it!

Rest & Be Well.

Motivate

Day Twenty: Pass Your Tests

I find it interesting that you want to experience the next level in your life - you want to start a family, start a business, travel the world and do all these great things, but then have such a hard time passing your own tests. It would be absurd for someone to believe that they should graduate or be promoted within their careers for simply showing up, right?

Unlike the sports team that you were a part of in elementary school, life doesn't hand out participation trophies. In order for you to experience the next level in your life, you must recognize the tests that life is giving you, study and do your best to pass. You often say, "God keeps testing me in this area of my life", but how many tests have you taken, answered the questions correctly and still received a failing grade? None, I'm sure. The reason that you keep being assigned the same test is because you're not passing it.

Let me tell you about my experience to further break down what I mean. I used to be, to say the least "a bit confrontational". Whoever wanted it, could get it, anywhere. I did not care! So I was always placed in situations which tested me in this specific area of my life. I eventually realized that the circumstances weren't my problem but it was my attitude and response towards the circumstances. Once I realized that this was a test that I needed to pass, I was faced again with someone who "wanted it" and I took the high road, leading me to unlock the door of a new opportunity.

Of course, once I passed that test, I started to become a bit full of myself. Now, I was no longer "the queen of confrontation". I had now become "the queen of condescending". Boy, did that get annoying fast! Yes, I was no longer yelling at anyone but my tone was so nasty that I may as well had been. With my new found awareness and understanding that my journey is a series of doors which I must unlock with my heart, I had to do a heart check and pass another test.

What tests are you failing within your life? _____

_____

_____

What has failing this/these test(s) kept you from? _____

_____

Develop a response to the test before it arrives again. Practice your response daily so that it becomes embedded in your psyche.

Which of the three principles will you rely on today?

- **Rules**

- **Realness**

- **Reflection**

How will this principle be of assistance to you? _____

_____

Rise & Be Great.

Meditate

Night Twenty: Pass Your Tests

Similar to formal schooling, tests are designed to strengthen you within a particular area. They're not created to break you down or stop you in your tracks. As long as you're encountering your tests and thinking "woe is me" instead of "victory", they will become recurring themes within your life - cycles. I want you to take tonight's meditation as an opportunity to _reflect._ Have you encountered a situation you're tired of seeing, but it just won't seem to go away? Is it in your finances? Your relationships? Your health?

_____

_____

Identify these things and then think about your attitude towards them. When you go into battle, are you prepared for the fight? When you face this test, have you immersed yourself in the material enough to pass it? _____

_____

What can you do to prepare for this test? _____

_____

If you do not prepare what will be your outcome? _____

_____

If you prepare as best as you can, what could you potentially learn

or earn? _____

_____

Meditate on your capability to pass this test the next time. Everything you need is already within you to conquer this feat, you just have to commit.

Rest & Be Well.

Motivate

Day Twenty-One: Immerse Yourself

As you and I end this journey of scheduled daily motivation and meditation, I ask that this not be the end. I encourage you to fill your life with people who will lift you up. Make decisions that will guide you towards your destiny. Listen to music that empowers you. Read material that brings you to a new level of consciousness and follow the direction of leaders who stretch you to reach your full potential. I pray that this journey does not come to an end, but that it instead creates a path for a new beginning for your life. I want nothing more than for you to eliminate every whisper of doubt that tells you that you're not capable. I want you to conquer every fear that has hindered you from trying new things. I want you to learn more about yourself and the world around you. I want you to love without limits. I NEED you to love without limits. Free yourself from shame. Free yourself from society's expectations of you. Free yourself from past trauma. Immerse yourself in the idea that you belong here. Choose people, places and things that remind you of that.

Reflect on this twenty-one day journey of rules, realness and reflection and allow yourself to experience redemption.

Redemption:

1. The action of saving or being saved from sin, error or evil.

2. The action of gaining or regaining possession of something in exchange for payment, or clearing a debt.

I want you to understand and believe that moving forward, you are new. Your habits, your thoughts about your circumstances, your feelings about yourself, and your behaviors are new. You have cleared the debt of your past shortcomings and it is now time to immerse yourself in everything that will help you to manifest the individual that you were purposed to become.

Do not put this book aside with the notion that the themes which appeared in it will not appear again within your everyday life. This is more than just a book. This is a *tool* and a *resource* for you to have the ability to coach yourself through all of life's situations. Depression cannot have you; anxiety has no place in your life. Un-forgiveness and low self-esteem were only things that existed because of your limited awareness of who you are and who's you have always been.

As I motivate you one last time, I ask you to choose life in all that you do and drown yourself in it.

Thoughts become things. What thoughts will you immerse yourself in? _____

_____

What book will you read next? _____

_____

Choose one theme from this book that you will take with you for the rest of your life.

Which of the three principles will you rely on today?

- **Rules**

- **Realness**

- **Reflection**

How will this principle be of assistance to you? _____

_____

Rise & Be Great.

Meditate

Night Twenty-One: Immerse Yourself

It's not over just yet. Will you drown yourself in the future that you want to manifest or will you choose to allow today to alter your faith towards the purpose that was designed for you?

I want you to not only immerse yourself for one hour, for one day, for one month…not even year will do. You must create the life you want by choosing the things that will birth that life. As you carry out your decisions daily, understand that the sum of them is what your life will become. Every decision you make in opposition of that life will set you back. And yes, some setbacks are designed to give you an opportunity for a major comeback, but life is going to throw you enough of those curve balls. Why create them for yourself?

As you and I spend the last time meditating together, I want you to identify which decisions are detouring you and setting you back?

Write yourself a letter tonight to add it to this book. I want you to embrace everything that you are and everything that you have the power to become. I want you to brag on yourself more than just a little in this present moment and speak about your future as though you are already there.

Dear (insert your name),

Start with affirmations, brag on yourself: (Example: You are enough, etc.)

Next, identify your weak areas and a solution to those problems: (If you struggle with commitment then it's imperative that you create daily schedules for your life.)

Next, lay to rest who you used to be with the thoughts, ideas and things that no longer serve you. (Depression has no power in your life; you will eliminate the toxic decisions that contribute to that and seek out the necessary help to maintain your mental health.)

List your sources of strength that you will rely on.

Celebrate your future as if you are already there. Speak about yourself in present tense, enjoying the bliss of love, success and freedom.

Continue to Rise & Be Great. Continue to Rest & Be Well.

You will need to them both in order to survive. But you will have to be intentional about them both in order to thrive.

END NOTES

1. https://www.wtsp.com/article/life/tampa-mama-ways-to-get-organized-in-the-new-year/67-45047351

2. https://www.fundera.com/blog/what-percentage-of-small-businesses-fail

3. https://www.independent.co.uk/life-style/love-sex/how-the-chance-you-breaking-up-with-your-partner-changes-as-your-relationship-goes-on-a6939856.html

4. https://www.neuronation.com/science/benefits-of-smiling

About the Author

A certified coach who specializes in transforming perspectives, Lanasia Angelina motivates individuals to rise above the confines of societal paradigms that diminish one's self-worth and esteem. A natural-born leader and trailblazer, Lanasia guides others into living their best lives by helping them to create balance, efficiency and a culture of success. Devoted to achieving spiritual and mental wellness, writing has allowed Lanasia to expand her reach. As an author, she utilizes storytelling to inspire through relatable experiences. By encouraging readers to reset and expand their boundaries, she honors her mission to promote personal and professional growth in a convenient way.

Visit www.lanasiaangelina.com for additional information.